THE MAGIC OF
TOPSAIL
ISLAND

Lindsay McAllister Zarse

D1227919

Illustrated by
Brian Martin

BEACH GLASS
BOOKS

Book Design by Brian Martin

Library of Congress Cataloging-in-Publication Data applied
for
ISBN-13: 978-0-61539-974-4
ISBN-10: 0-61539-974-6

Printed in the United States of America
October 2010

First Printing

beachglassbooks.com

THE MAGIC OF
TOPSAIL ISLAND

For Micah
(SHMILY?)

CONTENTS

~~~~~~

1

~~~~~~

I Don't Want To Go!

Riley anxiously watched the last few minutes tick off the clock over the blackboard. It was the last day of school before summer break and Isabelle, Riley's best friend and next-door neighbor, had invited Riley to spend a whole week with her family in the Outer Banks.

"Ring!" Riley raced out of the classroom and quickly boarded the school bus. The other students seemed to take forever to get on the bus. What was taking

everyone so long? Finally, the bus driver closed the door, pulled out of the loop and turned on to Academy Road.

The ride home felt like an eternity. Riley watched as the other students slowly unloaded at their stops. She waited as patiently as she could while the bus driver told each student she would see them next year and to have a wonderful summer in the meantime. When the driver pulled up to Riley's driveway, Riley was already up and waiting at the bus door. "My, you sure are ready to begin your summer, aren't you?" asked the driver. Riley smiled, bounded off the bus and ran down the driveway— screaming for her mother the whole way.

"Mom! Mom, where are you?" Riley yelled.

"I'm right here—loading the car," her mother answered.

"Mom!" Riley ran over to her mother. Almost out of breath, she announced, "Isabelle asked me to go to the beach with her for the whole week!"

"That's wonderful, honey; we can talk about it as soon as we get back from our trip. We need to leave soon, so hurry and get ready," her mother responded.

Riley looked heartbroken, "But Mom, Isabelle is leaving today, too,"

"I'm sorry, sweetie," her mother said sympathetically, "but you know this is our family's annual trip to Topsail Island. You won't be able to go with Isabelle."

"That's not fair! I don't want to go to Topsail! I want to go with Isabelle," a frustrated Riley said.

"Unfortunately, it is not up for discussion," her mother continued. "Besides, Topsail is a magical place."

Riley felt her frustration building as she entered the house. She flung her backpack onto the sofa and stomped her way up the stairs and into her room. After slamming her door shut, Riley pulled out a large red duffle bag from her closet. Books, dolls and video games were tossed angrily into the bag. When she was confident she had packed enough entertainment for the week, Riley headed down to the car where her mother and father were waiting.

As she sat in the back seat of the car, Riley thought about all the fun Isabelle would be having without her. She also thought about what her mother had said — about Topsail being a magical place. Riley thought to herself, "I do not see anything magical about it. It's just another beach."

The hum of the tires hitting the road coupled with the rhythm of the car itself helped Riley fall asleep.

2

~~~~~~

Serenity Point

Riley awoke just as her father pulled up to the beach house in Serenity Point. As much as she hated to admit it, this beach house was particularly beautiful. While her parents unloaded the car, Riley took a look around the inside of the house. She noticed the master bedroom had a balcony overlooking the sound side of the island.

"What a cool room," she thought. Given that this was the largest room in the house, though, it would clearly be the one where her parents would sleep. So Riley decided to check out the rest of the house. The second bedroom was equally as nice. Colorful fish paintings were on the wall, and this room, too, had its own, smaller balcony.

As she turned to leave the bedroom, Riley noticed a loft high off the living room. She climbed the wooden ladder to the top and found a pull-out futon.

Riley called out, "Hey, Mom, may I sleep up here?"

"I don't see why not," responded her mother.

Riley decided that she would make her own bed. She climbed back down the ladder and retrieved a set of bed sheets from the car. As she spread the sheets over the futon mattress, Riley noticed a small window in the loft that overlooked the ocean. A full moon shining down lit up the whole sea. It was breathtakingly beautiful.

Riley was tired from her long day. She lay down on her soft sheet and smiled a half smile. Maybe this will not be so bad

after all she thought. She drifted off to
sleep.

The next morning the family's two
dogs, Sir Houston and Lady Maritime, were
pacing back and forth just beneath the loft.
Riley heard her mother making coffee in
the kitchen and decided she might as well
get out of bed. She could always take a nap
later if she wanted.

"Well, good morning!" Riley's mother
exclaimed as Riley entered the room. "I was
just about to take the dogs for a walk on the
beach. Would you like to join us?"

Still upset about not getting to go
with Isabelle, Riley wanted to say no. But
she reluctantly agreed. There was probably

nothing else to do, anyway. She slipped on her flip-flops and was out the door.

Once on the beach, Riley tried not to have fun. She tried not to enjoy herself. It was just so hard not to smile while watching Maritime and Houston. They splashed in the surf and raced up the beach chasing seagulls. The dogs were in heaven, and as much as Riley hated to admit it, Topsail Island was pretty incredible. Riley reached down to pick up a shell at the same time Maritime was bounding into the surf.

Down they went, Riley laughing the whole time. She tried to stop herself, but it was too late. She was having fun. In fact,

she was having a lot of fun.

All of a sudden, Riley's mother

stopped walking.

3

~~~~~~~

The Nest

Riley looked up and saw large tire tracks heading from the ocean up towards the dunes. She was puzzled. What kind of car could have driven out of the ocean?

"Oh, Riley, look!" her mother said. "A mother turtle must have come ashore to lay her eggs last night!"

Riley was excited. She loved sea turtles. There was a small crowd of beach walkers gathering around the area where the tracks ended. Riley assumed they were looking at the nest. She wanted to look, too.

"Mom, lets go up there and see the nest," she said.

As they approached the dunes, Riley noticed two sea turtle hospital volunteers kneeling by the nest. One was saying the nest was far too close to the water. It was in danger of being washed away when the tide came in later that day. The pair decided the nest had to be moved.

The first volunteer informed the onlookers of what had to be done. She asked the group to look around for a large shell. Although she did not know why it was needed, Riley stepped forward and held out the shell she had pulled from the surf, "Like this?" she asked.

"Perfect!" exclaimed the volunteer. "When we are required to move nests for safety reasons, we take great care to insure our nest resembles the mother's nest as much as possible. Digging with the shell instead of a human hand makes the new nest more like the original."

Riley watched as one volunteer headed up closer to the dunes and began digging with her shell. The second volunteer carefully uncovered the nest and removed each egg one at a time and very slowly placed it into a bucket. Riley had never seen turtle eggs in real life before.

"This is amazing" she thought. The turtle eggs looked just like ping-pong balls!

After all ninety-six eggs had been collected and counted; the bucket was carried up to the new nest.

The eggs were gently placed into their new home at the base of the dune. Riley was thrilled that she could see what the nest looked like before it was covered with sand. She watched the volunteers sweep sand over the nest.

"Mom, why are they not patting the sand down?" inquired Riley.

"I am not sure, honey," responded her mother.

The first volunteer heard the exchange and had the answer: "A mother turtle is not able to pat down the sand over the nest; she uses her flippers to cover the eggs with sand. We want the new nest to be as much like the old one as possible. That means we cannot pat the sand down either."

Once the nest was covered, one of the volunteers drove four wooden stakes into the sand around it, forming a square. The stakes were tied together with orange tape. A sign was then placed in front, warning on-lookers to keep out.

The crowd dissipated. Riley and her mother headed home to the beach house.

"What took you guys so long?" asked Riley's father, as Riley brought Sir Houston into the house.

"Oh, Dad, it was amazing!" began Riley. "We found sea turtle tracks and a nest and the nest had to be moved and we got to see the eggs and…"

"Whoa, slow down, Princess," said her father. Riley smiled; her dad had called her that since she was a baby.

"You can tell me all about it at breakfast. Who wants to go to the Beach Shop?"

The Beach Shop was the family's favorite breakfast spot. Riley always

ordered the French toast. During breakfast,
Riley filled her father in on the morning's
events.

  After eating, Riley's father noted that
her week had started out quite nicely. "And
I will bet it gets even better as the week goes
on."

4

~~~~~~~~~

A Surprise Visitor

Riley's week, she had to admit, was a wonderful one. She spent her mornings walking the dogs on the beach while her mother looked for sea glass. Sometimes she looked. During the week, the two found many unique pieces in four different colors: green, aquamarine, white and brown. There were 212 pieces in different shapes and sizes.

Riley's afternoons were filled with body surfing, building sand castles and visiting the sea turtle hospital. Riley especially liked the sea turtles, most of which were loggerheads being rehabilitated for release back into the ocean. After dinner, Riley's father took them all for ice cream cones and a walk on the pier.

On the last night of their stay, Riley was enjoying her ice cream as her family was finishing their pier walk. Her mother commented on how pretty the sea looked and decided the three should spend some time on the beach watching the sun set. Riley's father went back to the beach house for a couple of beach chairs and a blanket.

Riley sat on the blanket, finishing her ice cream and thought, "maybe this trip wasn't such a bad idea." A full day of playing on the beach had left her exhausted. So she rested on the blanket and listened to the waves crashing on the shore. Soon she was fast asleep.

Suddenly, Riley awoke to a soft digging sound. She glanced over her shoulder to see a magnificent sea turtle within inches of her blanket.

"Nice night."

Riley was shocked. Surely the sea turtle could not talk.

"What a pleasant breeze—don't you think?"

"D-did you say something?" Riley
asked.

"Just commenting on the breeze, it's
such a beautiful night," responded the turtle.
"Oh, I'm sorry. How rude of me. My name
is Beasley. What is yours?"

"Riley," she replied in disbelief. Was
she actually talking to a turtle?

"I should really come up here more
often," Beasley said. "What about you—do
you come here often?"

"We have spent summers here ever
since I was a baby," Riley said. She still
could not believe she was conversing with
a turtle. Riley decided that this must be a
dream. But it was such a sweet dream she

allowed it to continue.

"What is it like down there?" asked Riley.

"In the ocean? Why, it is simply fabulous! Would you like to go?" asked Beasley. "I'm almost done laying these eggs. When I am through, I can take you to meet my friends!"

"I'd love to, but I am human. We cannot breathe underwater," Riley said.

Beasley replied, "Oh, sure you can — just grab a hold of my shell."

Riley glanced back at her parents who were talking quietly just a few feet away. Then she looked at Beasley and grabbed onto her shell.

5

~~~~~~~~

Pender and Onslow

Beasley started toward the water with Riley still holding on to her shell. Riley could feel the sand between her toes. She could even feel the cold water - this couldn't be a dream!

As she entered the water, Riley's legs were transformed into a shimmering green mermaid tail. Beasley dove further down with Riley still attached. A school of small fish went by. Beasley was about to have a jellyfish snack when suddenly a pair of seahorses rapidly approached.

"Beasley! Oh, Beasley, thank goodness you are back!" they cried.

"Calm down, calm down," replied Beasley. "Riley, this is Pender and Onslow—two very dear friends who apparently have important news."

"It's Shmily! He's been getting weaker and weaker. Will you please come and help him?" asked Pender.

"Of course, and you can fill me in on the way," Beasley responded.

Riley and Beasley swam closely behind the seahorses and listened as Onslow explained the situation.

"Shmily's mouth is broken! He can't eat a thing — and you know how unhappy a hungry shark can be."

"Shark!?" Riley exclaimed, nervously. "I can't go with you! Sharks eat people!"

Beasley laughed, "Do not worry. Shmily is a vegetarian—always has been."

Pender continued, "His wife just made him some seaweed casserole and he won't eat a bite!"

"My," replied Beasley, "that certainly is not like Shmily at all. Seaweed casserole is his favorite dish."

The friends swam deeper into the sea.

Beasley pointed out many mystic treasures along the way. Coral reef, clown fish and oysters displaying their pearls. When the group swam over a particularly lumpy patch of sand, Riley gasped — noticing that the sand was moving with them.

"That's just Old Ray. He's a nice fellow, though he can be grumpy at times."

The sand cleared and a majestic stingray appeared.

"Perhaps, I would not be so grumpy if I was not constantly awakened by you youngins," Old Ray replied, "What is the rush, anyway?"

"It is Shmily," began Onslow, "his mouth is broken and we are on our way to help him."

"A broken mouth?" questioned Old Ray. "Whoever heard of such nonsense?"

"It is true," responded Pender. "He is even refusing to eat seaweed casserole."

"Well, then it must be serious," Old Ray said. "Never known old Shmily to turn down food — especially seaweed casserole. Since I am awake now, I might as well come along in case I can be of some help."

The crew continued on with their mission, Old Ray following closely behind. They had almost made it to the coral reef when Beasley shushed the group.

"Shhhh," said Beasley, "we are passing over Crabby Mike's place. We certainly don't want to wake him."

Once Beasley was sure they had all passed over Crabby Mike's residence and were no longer in earshot, she turned to Riley and said, "it is just a little farther."

6

~~~~~~

Shmily

The group approached a large, moaning shark.

"Shmily, Beasley is here to help," stated Pender.

"Your mouth certainly does not look broken to me," said Beasley, matter-of-factly.

"But it must be," responded Shmily, "every time I bite down, I can feel my heart-beat in my mouth and the most unbearable pain follows."

"That certainly is odd. When did you first notice this, Shmily?" asked a very confused sea turtle.

"To be honest, I am not entirely sure. I guess it all started about a week ago. I remember eating dinner with some friends and thinking that my mouth hurt a little. As time passed, it has done nothing but gotten progressively worse. Now it is simply awful."

Shmily gasped loudly, "Oh, no! You do not think my mouth is dying, do you? It must be! How will I eat? I will surely starve to death!" Shmily cried worriedly.

"Now wait just a minute. No sense in getting all worked up. Besides, I am sure your mouth is not dying," Beasley said. She was used to Shmily's overly dramatic nature. Beasley glanced around at her friends. The group was noticeably confused, all except Riley, who chuckled to herself as a smile crossed her face.

"Why are you smiling, Riley?" asked Beasley.

"Because it is not his mouth that is broken. It is probably just his tooth," responded Riley.

"What?" asked an even more confused Shmily.

"Your tooth. I bet you have a cavity in the spot where it hurts the most," answered Riley.

"Well, what is a cavity and how do I fix it?" Shmily asked.

"A cavity," started Riley, "is a small hole in your tooth that makes it really painful to eat. On land, when we get a cavity, it can be filled. But since we are in the ocean, it will most likely have to be pulled."

"Let's get to it then," said Shmily, "I am starving!"

"We have to figure out which tooth it is, first," noted Riley.

"If you open really wide, I can swim in and take a look," offered Pender.

Shmily opened his mouth as wide as he possibly could. Pender hesitantly swam in and took a look around. When Pender swam out, he announced, "It's the one on the back right. I can tell because there is swelling all around it."

Having figured out the problem, the group was now faced with trying to figure out how to get that tooth out. It was at that very moment the friends were approached by a rather crabby crab.

7

~~~~~~

A Not-So-Crabby Crab

"**W**hat is all the commotion about?"
Crabby Mike asked.

"Sorry, Mike, I guess we woke you
when we swam by. We were in such a hurry
to get to Shmily. He needs our help,"
Beasley replied.

"Is there anything I can do to help,
Shmily?" Mike asked.

"I bet Mike can get the tooth out for
Shmily!" Riley exclaimed. A smile crossed
her face.

"I would be happy to help my good friend, Shmily," said Mike. "Which one is it?"

"I checked it out, and it appears to be the back right tooth on the bottom," Pender said.

"OK, Shmily, lets get that tooth out," said Mike. Shmily happily opened wide. Crabby Mike swam in and wrapped his large claw around the problem tooth.

He gave a good, hard yank. The tooth went flying out of Shmily's mouth and landed on the sea floor.

"Wow!" Riley shouted. "That worked great! And it was so nice of you to help. You are not nearly as crabby as I had imagined."

Now a big smile crossed Beasley's face.

"We call him 'crabby' because he is a crab. Crabby Mike is our friend," she said.

"The only reason we did not want to wake him is because he had a long day at the Surf City Pier."

"Yeah," replied Mike, "I like to circle the pier while the fishermen are there with their bait — it is a great place to eat."

Shmily, who was also smiling, announced, "Speaking of eating, I am heading home to eat some seaweed casserole. Thanks for the help, my friends!"

Shmily hurried home, as did the rest of the group. Beasley turned to Riley and said, "I guess I better get you back, too."

"Yes," replied Riley looking toward the sea floor. "But before we go, do you think it would be OK if I took Shmily's tooth with me?"

"I don't see why not. He certainly does not want it," Beasley answered.

Riley picked up the tooth from the ocean floor and then reached back and grabbed onto Beasley.

The pair swam to the surface. As they neared the beach, Riley thought about her grand adventure and her new friends. Beasley helped her out of the ocean. Riley's legs had returned. Sleepily, Riley crawled onto the blanket and was falling asleep.

"It is getting late, " she heard her mother say — or thought she did. As her mother gathered the chairs, Riley felt her father scoop her up, blanket and all. He carried her back to their beach house and up the stairs to her bed in the loft.

8

~~~~~~~

More Excitement

The next morning, Riley awoke to the smell of bacon. On the last morning of their beach week, the family always had a large breakfast. Riley remembered the night before. Had it all been a dream? It felt so real, but it could not have been, could it?

Riley pondered this as she rose out of bed. She felt something in her hand. She looked down to see a large shark tooth. It was Shmily's! It was not a dream, after all!

Excitedly, Riley rushed down to breakfast. She showed the shark tooth to her mother and father.

"That is quite a tooth, Riley," her father said.

"Yes, it is, and it is part of the magic of Topsail," Riley announced. A big smile crossed her face.

Riley enjoyed her big breakfast even though she was saddened at the thought of leaving the island.

"Mom," Riley began, "do you think we could take one more walk on the beach before we have to head home?"

"I think that is a great idea, Riley. Plus, I am sure the dogs will appreciate a long walk before a long car ride home," her mother said.

Riley's father grabbed the leashes from the counter and hooked them to Sir Houston and Lady Maritime.

Maritime, always very excitable, immediately started pulling Riley toward the door.

Riley giggled at her puppy.

Maritime's tail seemed to be wagging the silly puppy's whole body.

Riley's family climbed the steps to the beach access and decided to walk toward the Jolly Roger Pier. Once again, the dogs bounced around in the surf and took delight in scaring the seagulls into flight. The salty sea breeze felt wonderful on Riley's face. She watched as her mother reached down to rescue a beautiful piece of aquamarine sea glass from the rapidly approaching waves.

"Look!" shouted Riley's father. He was a few feet ahead.

"Wow!" exclaimed Riley's mother, "Two in one week!"

"Pretty impressive," her father said.

"We must have just missed her," her mother said.

Riley looked up to see the large tire-like tracks heading out of the ocean and up the beach. Then Riley looked down where she was standing. This was the exact spot where the family had been sitting last night.

"Beasley," she thought to herself.

"We have to come back to see the babies," cried Riley. "Please can we?"

"Wait, you want to come back?" asked her father. "You? The girl who did not even want to come to Topsail Island wants to come back?"

"Dad, that was before I learned about the magic of Topsail. Plus, I want to be here to see Beasley's children hatch," said Riley.

"Whose children?" asked her mother. Oops. Her parents had not met Beasley. They would probably never believe her tale. So Riley responded, "I just thought the mother turtle should have a name, so I decided to call her Beasley."

"Well, that is a wonderful idea, sweetie," her mother said, smiling.

"Both ideas are wonderful," her father said. "The name for the mother turtle and the suggestion for a return trip at the end of the summer."

Riley and her mother smiled at each other. Then, the smile ran off her mother's face. It was replaced by a puzzled expression.

"Why in the world are there so many turtle tracks leading to and from the ocean? Her mother asked. "Maybe 'Beasley' was dragging something else into the water?"

Riley smiled. "Oh, I think it is probably just more of that Topsail magic you and Dad are always talking about."

About the Author

When not at her family's Topsail Island beach home, Lindsay Zarse lives outside Richmond, Virginia, with her husband and daughter. After graduating from Old Dominion University, Lindsay received a Master's Degree in Education from Penn State University. She is a high school teacher in Chesterfield County, Virginia.